A SAILING PRIMER

A SAILING

NEW YORK   1978   ATHENEUM

PRIMER

Harvey Frommer &
Ron Weinmann

PHOTOGRAPHS BY HARVEY FROMMER AND RON WEINMANN

Library of Congress Cataloging in Publication Data

Frommer, Harvey.
  A sailing primer.

  1. Sailing. I. Weinmann, Ron, joint author.
II. Title.
GV811.F9 1978   797.1'24   77-13431
ISBN 0-689-10841-9

DEDICATION

*To our first mates, Myrna Frommer and
Merle Weinmann, and to the rest of
the crew: Jennifer, Freddy, Ian, Scott,
and Dennis. Special thanks to Arthur Kramer
for taking over the tiller.*

Introduction

AS A CHILD you might have taken Popsicle sticks and placed them together and attached a piece of paper. As long as the wind was behind the piece of paper this makeshift vessel was able to move forward in a straight line. That was sailing.

As a child you might have placed a wooden toy boat beside you while you took a bath. The toy boat would float. You might have moved the water about, and the boat would move forward. That was sailing.

The gentle thrill and excitement of control of an object in the water has stayed with many children who have grown up. They still sail.

Some sail for the smell of the spray and the feel

of the wind, the romance of the water and the liquid sun. Others sail for therapeutic reasons—to get away from it all, to have a psychological release. Still others sail because they have to—for the feel of a boat on the water.

But whether it is the teenager with his $600 boat or the business executive who during the workweek is dressed in a three-piece Brooks Brothers suit and wears cutoff jeans and sneakers without socks on the weekend, all those who sail are part of a fraternity.

This fraternity shares the sea and the sailing and the experience. There are very few snobs. Everyone waves to one another. Whether it's a millionaire in his $500,000 racing machine or a youngster with a used dinghy hull, all those who sail share the unwritten code of the sea—help each other.

Until about 1945, sailboats were few in number compared to today. But after the war, changes in materials and methods of manufacture made sailing a less expensive sport. Fiberglass was introduced. Boats were mass produced easily. They were faster, more economical boats. Wood plank construction was replaced. All the builder needed was a mold of the desired hull.

Synthetic sail material replaced the cotton duck that had been used for hundreds of years. Cotton rotted, stretched, and shrank. Nylon and then Dacron sails were lighter in weight and stretch resistant, and they lasted longer.

Aluminum masts replaced wooden ones. Stainless steel rigging replaced stays and shrouds made of galvanized material. And with these changes in materials came more and more changes in the styles and the shapes and the classes (types) of sailboats. Today there are more than a thousand classes of sailboats. There is a type of boat for every need, for every taste, for every pocketbook.

As the world has become more complex, more and more people have turned away, if only for a while, from life on land and welcomed the other life of sailing on the sea. Whole families have been drawn closer together in the common experience of sailing. Other individuals have gone off by themselves and forgotten the cares of the day in the lapping waves and the gentle dip and flow of a boat under sail. Some of the famous figures in American life sail: Walter Cronkite, Bill Buckley, Dick Van Dyke.

Sailing has much value. In a world that is becoming more and more concerned about its natural resources and the problem of pollution, sailboats and the increase in sailing are good signs. Sailboats don't pollute. They don't drink up precious oil. It's a fact that in some sections of some countries of the world, only sailboats are allowed. Powerboats, which pollute, are banned. We may yet see this situation developing in the United States. With the cost of gas and oil rising annually and the dangers of pollution to our rivers and streams a national concern, sailing is a way out of the problem.

Another real value of sailing is the respect and attention to the elements that it breeds into the sailor. One who would sail well must know something about science, about mathematics, about tides and winds, water dynamics and physics. The true sailor learns to work with these things, to pay attention to them, to get enjoyment from them, to respect them.

Sailing is simple. Sailing is difficult. Sailing is safe. Yet for the foolhardy it can be dangerous. It is a seasonal activity in some sections of this country and a year-round joy in other areas. It is most of all a way of life that you can enjoy through all the years of your life, alone or with those you care about.

We view this book as a tool for beginning sailors. It could have been five times the size, but nothing of basic importance has been left out. Careful reading and rereading of this book and application of its information will make it possible for you to sail safely and efficiently. So, let's sail away. . . .

Contents

1. THE ABC'S OF SAILING   3

*Types of Boats; Getting a Boat; Every Boat Has to Have
a Home; Maintaining the Boat; Safety and Emergencies;
Capsizing; Rules of the Road—Right of Way*

2. NOW YOU'RE READY   20

*Basic Vocabulary of the Sea; Getting Under Way and
Making Sail; Anchoring; Docking*

3. THE ART AND SCIENCE OF SAILING   39

*Aerodynamics and Water Dynamics; Points of Sailing;
The Traveler and Boom Vang: Points of Sailing Aids;
Steering and the Tiller; Turning Maneuvers: Tacking and
Jibing; Points of Sailing—Summary Comments*

4. SAILING WITH THE SENSES   63

The Five Senses and Sailing; Weather and Barometric Pressure Signs for the Senses; Balance: Hull and Crew; Balance via the Mainsheet, Traveler, and Jib; Shaping of Sails

5. TIPS FROM THE PROS   83

GLOSSARY   90

A SAILING PRIMER

1. The ABC's of Sailing

ANY SAILOR worth his salt will tell you that the basics of sailing must be understood before you can actually sail. This chapter presents bread-and-butter, practical information that a beginning sailor needs.

TYPES OF BOATS

Sailboats are classified according to their size and the way their sails are arranged. There is an enormous variety of sailboats from the simplest one-sailed catboat to the oceangoing schooner. As a beginning sailor, however, you will probably be considering a small boat that is easy to sail and comparatively inexpensive. A catboat with a single mast forward in the boat and a single sail is a popular choice. It may be as small as eight to twelve feet, small enough for easy handling. It will probably lack a head (toilet facilities), railings, and lifelines. It is not always self-righting. But it is a true planing boat, riding the surface of the water like a surfboard. In seas of four feet or more, however, the small size and light weight of the catboat could cause it to slow down and become a displacement boat, pushing the water on all sides.

For the beginner, it can be a marvelous little boat. Its size, convenience in docking and management, and economical advantages make it well worth considering.

A sloop is another popular type of sailboat. It is sometimes larger than the catboat, with a mast further back toward the middle and at least two sails. It is also more expensive and more complicated to sail, generally needing two or more individuals to handle it. Sloops are good cruising boats. They usually have sleeping accommodations, heads, and are family or group oriented. Usually sloops have lifelines and railings and are self-righting, which makes it almost impossible for them to capsize.

Generally sloops operate by displacing water. What happens is that the sloop actually pushes the water on all sides, displacing its own weight. Yet in certain situations sloops can plane or surf on the water. Sloops usually have round bottoms with a fixed extension protruding from the bottom known as a keel, but sometimes have centerboards. Smaller boats such as Sunfish and Laser have flat bottoms and do not have keels. Like the catboat, these are nondisplacement or planing boats and are also good choices for the beginning sailor.

GETTING A BOAT

With more than a thousand classes (types) of boats to pick from, your first task is to limit your choice. Comfort, available mooring and launching facilities, upkeep, the possibility that you may wish to race the boat—all of these have to be evaluated.

There are two main methods of getting a boat: buy a boat, new or used; or build one, either from plans or from scratch without plans.

The simplest way to get your boat is to buy it

new—it's the safest way and also the most expensive. If you go the route of buying a used boat, be cautious. Question why the boat is being sold. Have it checked out thoroughly by someone you trust who knows about boats, or by a surveyor, before handing over your money. You can get a good deal on a used boat. You can also get taken.

If you decide to build a boat, the easier method is to put it together from kit plans. These are directions produced by some of America's best boat-building firms. No previous boat-building experience is required to follow the step-by-step plans. Prams, approximately eight feet long, are perhaps the most practical small boats that you can build. You can buy all the parts in a kit and fit them together.

The cheapest and most satisfying way to get a boat is to build one from scratch. Naturally, don't do this unless you have design skill and boat-building experience. The effort will be time consuming, but it will be a creative experience that will bring you close to the boat you will eventually sail.

EVERY BOAT HAS TO HAVE A HOME

A place has to be provided for your boat when you are not sailing it. And there has to be a method for you to get your boat in and out of its sailing life.

There are two main categories of "homes": dry sailing and wet sailing.

Dry sailing means keeping the boat ashore and bringing it to the water by one of several methods. Beaching consists of simply tying the boat down to land and having it remain safe from water even with flood tides about. Car topping has you placing the boat on top of your car and bringing it down to the water, where it is set up and made ready to sail away. The boat, of course, must be small enough for this; boats heavier than three hundred pounds pose a problem unless you're in shape for Olympic weight lifting. Trailering involves attaching a boat to the rear of a car and pulling it down to water. This method is useful for you to transport your boat anywhere in the country. Check with traffic laws or the police; trailers are not permitted on some highways. Craning is the method used by most yacht clubs;

Boats at home on a mooring.

Boat at home in a slip.

boats are pulled out of the water by a crane and stacked on land.

Wet sailing means keeping the boat in the water; you travel to where the boat is. There are two methods of wet sailing. Slip (docking) is where the boat is tied up to a series of poles enabling you to have a stationary boat that does not experience any bumping or damage to its sides. Mooring, a fixed mushroom anchor is dropped into the water on a length of chain considerably longer than the depth of water at the highest tide. The longer the anchor stays in the mud, the better mooring it is. A buoy is attached to the mooring cable and floats on the water's surface. The boat is then fastened to the buoy. This is the best of homes for sailboats—but you must have a boat to take you to your mooring, unless you're a real good swimmer and one who does not mind roughing it. Those who belong to a yacht club do the mooring bit in style. They get taken out to their boat by launch.

The decision as to the type of home and the way you get to your boat will be governed by such things as type of boat, finances, convenience, and personal preference. The information presented here should help sharpen your decision-making powers.

Maintaining the boat can be fun.

MAINTAINING THE BOAT

A sailboat is an investment. Whether it's your first boat, a new boat you've just gotten, or an old boat, there are several things that must be done to keep it in top condition.

Sanding. A boat must become part of the water that it spends so much time on. In skiing a coat of wax helps you glide faster over snow; any coating on the underside of a boat only slows you down. A modular layer of bubbles is created that causes friction. This wax should be removed. The best way to do this it to sand the bottom lightly, using wet sandpaper. This removes the gellcoat, the shiny fiberglass surface. If this is not done, bottom paint will not stick. Use wet paper 220–600.

Painting. Undersides of boats get a lot of wear and tear. Boat bottoms are helped a great deal by antifouling paint, which contains chemicals that are poisonous to barnacles and marine growths. It is available in a variety of attractive colors such as vinyl red, submarine copper bronze, bright blue, and green. If you dry sail your boat (store it out of the water), there is no need for antifouling paint. If you wet sail (store the boat in the water), there is definitely a need for antifouling paint. This is especially true in saltwater sailing, where there is maximum fouling, as opposed to freshwater sailing, which incurs minimum fouling. Oddly enough, the cleaner the water, the worse the fouling. This is because polluted water hinders marine growth.

Waxing. The major problems that affect fiberglass boats come from discoloration from the sun. The solution to these problems lies in waxing the boat.

The operating rule is to apply wax to all surfaces on a boat, even a new one. But don't apply wax to the bottom or the nonskid surfaces or you'll change nonskid to skid with damaging results. Thus, nonskid decking, which is generally a nubby tweed or a vinyl sand floor, should not be waxed. These places are not dance floors. They are surfaces for you to keep your footing in order to manage your boat. In the summer, wax at least once a month. Get a friend to wax along with you. It is also important to apply a coat of wax to the boat prior to winter storage. Allow the wax to remain on as protection all through the winter.

Winter Storage. Boats can be stored in a boat yard, either outdoors or indoors. Outdoors is cheaper, but you must cover the boat with a waterproof tarpaulin or some other covering to protect it against the elements. Make sure the covering permits ventilation to eliminate mold and mildew. Indoor storage gives you a chance to get to the open boat to do some work.

Stored boats should be clean and scrubbed down. It is a good time for you to make notes on repair work that might be needed. Some of these odd jobs will make pleasant ways for you to pass the winter hours thinking of sailing days ahead.

SAFETY AND EMERGENCIES

The most experienced sailors will tell you that safety on a boat and anticipation of emergencies rank among the most important aspects of sailing. Respect for the sea and common sense are two essentials of sailing safety. There are a few prime rules that should be followed to make your time on the water free of panic and full of enjoyment.

1. The Coast Guard requires that a boat must be equipped with a life preserver for each person who sails on it. Pride and intelligence dictate that a life preserver should be put on as soon as the wind picks up. The best swimmers, the most experienced sailors, wear life preservers when the wind picks up. To a sailor, the person without a life preserver in a 30-mile-an-hour wind is a fool.

2. Always follow the directions of the captain of the boat. That person is in charge. If you are told to stand on the windward side, stand there. You might not be too happy leaving a comfortable position, but the captain gives directions for the good of the boat.

Safety equipment.

The young lady at the helm is an accomplished swimmer, but she still wears a life preserver—not only for safety but peace of mind. Note the tiller extension which enables her to hike out and still maintain control of helm.

3. Don't show off. There is no reason to stand up and hang out on the bow, or to jump about or climb and show your athletic ability.

4. Be alert and keep your head. When the boom of the boat is being moved in jibing or tacking, be aware that unless you adjust your movement and position, you can wind up with a nasty headache or worse.

5. Resist the impulse to smoke on a boat. Smoking can be very dangerous, especially when you are taking on fuel at a gas dock or when there's gas on the boat. Fumes ignite and can cause an explosion on the boat.

6. Sea cocks are safety devices located at or below the waterline. The majority of them look like and function as faucets. Their main purpose is to control water flow in and out of the boat. Sea cocks should always be *closed* when not in use, or you could wind up with a flood. Sea cocks should be open if you have an engine on the boat and are using it. A closed sea cock does not allow water in to cool the engine, and you're liable to have a burned-out engine if the sea cock is not in the open or cooling position. Close sea cock on head if not in use.

7. All movable objects on a boat should be battened (anchored) down. Food, radios, flashlights,

all of these can become lethal objects if they are sent flying through the air in the close quarters of a boat.

8. Stock proper equipment. In addition to life preservers, an FM radio, a first-aid kit, a flashlight, and flares are very important. The radio is useful for weather reports. Information that a cold front is coming in indicates, for example, that excessive winds may be moving up. Flares are important to signal that you have a problem or emergency to other boats.

9. Never overload a boat with people or things. Sailboat space is carefully accounted for. Putting extra strain on a boat and cutting down on free movement can cause problems.

10. Finally, keep everything shipshape. Pride in sailing and safety go together. A sloppy boat is a problem boat.

CAPSIZING

A sometimes frightening but often common and not dangerous situation is finding yourself in the water when you didn't want to be there—your sailboat has capsized. The predicament is that of an overturned boat, sails in the water, hull in the vertical position, not horizontal as you would wish it to be.

If you are wearing your life preserver, you'll float and you'll have the extra margin of safety and comfort and freedom from fear that you will need. It is important for you to realize now that every sailor worthy of that name has been capsized at one time or another. Even champions in all types of boats have found themselves in the water when they didn't want to be there. It's part of the fun of sailing. Remember—even if you're in a self-righting boat —don't take chances.

If you are going to be a sailor on a dinghy type boat, you will probably experience capsizing. The experience is caused by excessive winds. If the wind speed is 0 to 8 mph, you won't capsize unless you are sailing poorly. Over that speed a boat can and usually will capsize unless it is sailed expertly.

If it happens and you're in the water, keep your head. The most important rule is to stay with the boat. Don't swim to shore. You may never get there. Swim to the keel and pull. Then stand on the keel. The excess weight (you) on the keel will make the boat right itself, and the sail and the mast will lift out of the water. Climb in and joke about your unexpected dip in the drink.

RULES OF THE ROAD—RIGHT OF WAY

Just as there are road traffic regulations, there are marine traffic regulations that have been set up to avoid collisions on the water. It is essential to know the traffic rules for the waters that you sail in. The prime rule is to avoid a collision. So even if you have the right of way, move away to avoid collision. In this way you won't wind up as Silas McVey did:

Here lie the bones of Silas McVey,
Who died defending his Right of Way—
He was right, dead right, as he sailed along,
But he's just as dead as if he'd been wrong.

With Silas in mind, here are five basic **RIGHT OF WAY RULES OF THE ROAD:**

1. A sailboat always has the right of way over a powerboat.

2. If there are two sailboats approaching each other, the one on the starboard tack always has the right of way.

18

3. If two boats are approaching each other on a starboard tack, the one that is leeward has the right of way.

4. A sailboat has the right of way only when it is under sail. Under power, it is treated as a powerboat.

5. Right of way is not applicable to freighters or commercial craft. They have a lot of difficulty with stopping distances. Sailboats are like fleas to them. Don't challenge or look for right of way as far as they are concerned. Get out of the way. Remember Silas McVey.

2. Now You're Ready

BASIC VOCABULARY OF THE SEA

Sailing has a language all its own. The *bow* is the front of the boat; the *stern* is the rear of the boat. *Fore, forward* indicate going to the front; *aft* indicates going to the rear. Facing forward, *starboard* is right and *port* is left.

Windward (weather) refers to the side of the boat from which the wind is blowing. *Lee* refers to the side of the boat that is away from the wind. A boat on the *port tack* has its sail on the right *(starboard)* while the wind is coming from the left *(port)*. A boat on *starboard tack* has its sail on the left *(port)* while the wind is coming from the right *(starboard)*.

Many parts make up a sailboat. The *hull* is the body of a boat. The *keel, centerboard, daggerboard,* is the extra underwater area of a boat that gives it stability, that keeps it on a straight line and prevents *leeway* (drifting). The steering wheel of a sailboat is called the *tiller*. It is connected to the *rudder,* which is located at the stern or under the hull and controls the course of a boat. The *centerline* is the imaginary line that divides the boat in half from the center of the bow to the center of the stern.

Spars are poles that support the sails. There are three main types of spars: *masts, booms,* and *gaffs.* The *mast* is a vertical spar that holds the sail. The *boom* is a spar to which the *foot* (bottom) of the main is attached. The *gaff* is a spar to which the *head* (top) of the sail is attached. The *boom* extends at right angles to *mast* and holds the sail straight out.

The *mainsail* is fastened to the back of the mast. A triangular sail called the *jib* is in front of the mast. Working together with the *mainsail,* the *jib* enables the boat to move faster. The spinnaker is a large sail mainly used for off-wind (when the wind is aft of the beam) sailing or racing. Most of the time it comes in bright colors for added style.

The *luff* is the front edge or end of a sail that faces the bow of the boat. The back end or edge of a sail that faces the boat's stern is called the *leech*. The *masthead pennant* is a flag located at the highest point of the boat, atop the sail. It indicates wind direction.

Rigging refers to all the lines and ropes used to control and support the sails. Effective and safe sailing is based partly on understanding and maintaining the rigging. The whistling sound through the sails that so delights sailors is the echo of wind vibration. It should be a sign to you that nature is at work. At least once a week, check for loosened rigging. Even though standing rigging is generally stainless steel, it can stretch and may need adjusting.

STANDING RIGGING is permanent. It holds the mast fore and aft and keeps it in an upright position. This is accomplished through the use of STAYS, which are lengths of wire or rope: The HEADSTAY runs from the top of the mast to the bow; the BACKSTAY runs from the top of the mast to the stern; the SHROUDS, generally two upper and four lower, run from the mast to the sides of the boat. All the stays attach to the hull of the boat via turnbuckles, threaded adjustable links.

An overall tuning concept applies to standing rigging. Some of the general principles are:

1. Headstay should be as tight as possible without distorting the fore and aft position of the hull. (Do not sail with a tight headstay in chop.)

2. Upper shrouds should be as tight as possible.

3. Lower shrouds should be moderately tight.

4. The mast should basically be in a perpendicular position to the waterline and the deck for most boats.

RUNNING RIGGING refers to the ropes, or wires that hoist, set, and trim sails. It must be constantly adjusted. The JIB HALYARD and MAIN HALYARD are ropes or wires used to raise and lower sails. The MAINSHEET and JIBSHEET are control lines used to trim or adjust sails. The TRAVELER is a metal rod track along which the MAINSHEET slides. The BOOM VANG is a line from the underside of the boom to the mast at deck level. These control the depth and position of the sails. The OUTHAUL is a line that holds and adjusts the mainsail at its foot. It controls the depth and flatness of sail: When the outhaul is eased, you will get a fuller sail; when the outhaul is tightened, you will get a flatter sail. The DOWNHAUL is a line that holds the sail down, and can move the draft in main-

Main sheet without traveler.

Main sheet with traveler.

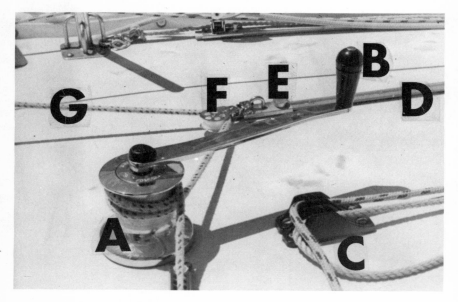

a) Winch b) Winch handle c) Clam cleats d) Genoa track e) Genoa car f) Genoa block g) Jib sheet.

a) Boom Vang b) Spinnaker halyard winch c) Cunningham d) Main-sheet e) Jib halyard winch.

sail forward.

There are many RUNNING RIGGING adjustments. You will discover, as you sail, they will eventually come as second nature to you.

There's a glossary at the back of this book that more completely describes the terms of sailing. Also terms used later on in this book will be explained as they are utilized. But with the knowledge of these basic terms and understanding of the illustrations, you can already be thinking and talking like a sailor. As the old song goes, "The thigh bone's connected to the knee bone . . ." and "The traveler's connected to the mainsheet, the mainsheet's connected to the boom, the boom's connected to the mast . . ."

GETTING UNDER WAY AND MAKING SAIL

There's a routine that must be mastered to insure you and your boat are out free and clear with the sun and the spray. The whole process may seem complicated; however, it's just a matter of attention to details, just a few minutes of time, but very important to insure clear sailing.

Your presailing action involves leaving your

Boarding the boat: One hand for safety and one for the boat. Step as close to centerline as possible.

estimated return time with a responsible person, checking out the local weather forecast, and checking to see that you have all the necessary equipment on the boat.

Board the boat always with one hand free. "One hand for yourself, and one for the ship," explains the old sailing expression. Step into the boat as close to the centerline as possible. This helps you to keep your balance. Remember that you're a sailor and not an acrobat; don't leap into the boat. You may break something, and it might be part of you. Secure all loose gear.

In a centerboard boat, the first step in making sail is accomplished by fully lowering the centerboard. Next rig the rudder and tiller. Sponge or pump dry the bilge (the curved part of the hull below the waterline).

Uncleat the mainsheet (a cleat is a device that holds a line secure). Allow enough slack for the boom to swing freely when the mainsheet goes up. Rig next the port and starboard jibsheets. Check out if the main and jib halyards will run free.

Halyard-mainsail attachment is next made. The foot is bent to the boom and stretched with the outhaul. Bend the luff to the mast. Insert battens (items that stiffen the edge of a sail). Cast off the downhaul on the boom.

At this point you should be ready to uncleat the buoy. Decide on a port or starboard tack.

Hoist the mainsail. Secure its halyard. Raise the jib and secure its halyard. If you're leaving from a dock, ready your paddle and push off. If you're leaving from a mooring, the mooring line can be used to swing the boat around to your choice of sailing direction. Note well: Never leave the dock area under sail. It is inconsiderate to others; and if there is no wind, it might be frustrating as well as nearly impossible.

Raising the sail.

31

Using Jib halyard winch.

Checking the sail.

ANCHORING

Some time on the water, you may wish to come to a stop—to fish, to swim, to eat, perhaps to pull up for the night and go to sleep. Anchoring is a key, but sometimes overlooked, part of helmsmanship. Mastering the art of anchoring is essential for sailing safety and comfort.

You have probably seen the romantic image of the sailor and the large anchor. A rope goes around and around in the air, and the anchor is tossed out into the swirling sea. It's almost as if the person doing the anchoring is getting ready to lasso a cow. This romantic image is a turnoff to a real sailor. It is, in fact, poor seamanship.

A valuable and necessary tool, an anchor should not be dropped or flung into the water. It should be gently placed over the side of a boat. You should also lay your anchor line out in the cockpit, then lay out the anchor and place it in the water. This will prevent you from the snafu of getting all tangled up in rope.

Anchors come in three different types: mud,

33

A Danford anchor.

A Plow anchor.

sand, and rock. Important differences exist among the three. A check with your dealer will give you the local knowledge about the type of anchor needed for your area. As a general rule, a thirty-foot boat requires an anchor weighing about 14 pounds.

Important anchoring hints include:

1. Protect the anchor line with chafing gear, especially in heavy weather. Simple split hose or canvas wrapped around the anchor cable will prevent chafing.

2. Don't pick an anchor spot too close to other boats. Wind shifts or tide turns may bring you closer to the other boats than you would wish. You could have trouble.

3. Make sure you have enough scope (length of anchor line between boat and anchor) so that the anchor will do what it is supposed to do—anchor the boat. For a lunchtime stop or a swim, the scope should be about five to one. If there's some wind, ten to one is better. (The ratio is best explained as follows: If the depth of the water is 30 feet, five-to-one scope is 150 feet.)

4. Take no chances guessing at the depth of the water. Geological charts have this information. If you don't have charts, markings that measure depth can be purchased. You can even make your own

markings by stretching out rope and marking off ten-foot distances with indelible ink.

5. A simple procedure for bringing the anchor in is to reduce the scope by pulling on the anchor rode (rope) until the bow of the boat is approximately directly above the anchor. Any upward motion on the rode should easily free the anchor.

6. Finally, anchoring is simple and mechanical. Don't take chances whith the type of anchor, the rules of anchoring, the depth of the water. You may be taking chances with your life.

DOCKING

Bringing a boat back after a pleasant time on the water is very much like parking a car. Reduced speed, easing into place, and putting the boat to bed in the reverse order you made sail are the simple procedures that are needed.

It is worth stressing that a boat that is docked must have some preparations made for protection. Bumpers are important. They prevent the sides of the boat from becoming marred or damaged. You can obtain pneumatic or canvas bumpers if your

Bumpers—docking protection keeping hull from scratching.

dock area does not have them. Tires are sometimes used, but these tend to run black dye against the fiberglass and mar the boat's beauty.

An excellent docking prep technique is to fend off with a springline. Add another line on the opposite side holding the boat away from the dock. This technique pulls the boat away from the dock and prevents banging or bumping from wind, wake, or powerboats.

3. The Art and Science of Sailing

AERODYNAMICS AND WATER DYNAMICS

Before you can really understand the nuts and bolts of helmsmanship, it is important that you grasp why a boat sails and how air and water and the boat intermingle to make for sailing.

Briefly, boats sail when the wind is behind them, and they are pushed along. This is the condition of running or sailing downwind. The sail should be trimmed at right angles to the wind to take advantage of this aerodynamic rule of sailing. The sail is thus able to get maximum resistance to the wind.

Another situation takes place when the boat

sails against the wind. Pressure comes against the windward side, pushing, while a pulling vacuum exists on the lee side. The wind blowing against the curved surface of the sail resembles the thrust that makes an airplane stay in the air. Sails should be 45 degrees from the wind to take advantage of this aerodynamic situation. The sails become an airfoil similar to the airplane wing.

Thus, the pushing and the pulling pressures on sails make it possible to sail a boat in many directions regardless of the direction in which the wind blows. However, there is an almost 90-degree area—45 degrees on each side of the wind—where sailing is not possible.

At the water dynamics level, two factors operate: drag and drive. The hull of a boat floats in the water—drags. Sufficient wind pressure overcomes the drag and makes the boat sail. If the wind is strong enough, it makes the boat drive. In some situations, a sailboat can almost lift off the water, driving, planing ahead.

In brief, that's how water and wind and boat all get together in the experience known as sailing.

The easiest way to determine the relationship of the wind to the setting of the sails is through the masthead pennant blowing against the sky on the top of the mast. Telltales, pieces of black knitting wool, attached to the main and jib are useful. Their blackness helps you see through the opaque white of the sails.

POINTS OF SAILING

Like so many other areas of human experience, sailing has undergone a revolution over the centuries. The boats of the eighteenth and nineteenth centuries did not have the abilities of the modern sloops and dinghies. They were limited by their riggings in what they could do on the water and what they could do with the wind.

There are stories about boats that took years to sail from China to America. In these romantic stories, it was said that these boats followed the trade winds. What this means is that most times the old sailing boats had to place themselves in positions where their sails had to catch and use the wind that was behind them. The routes they followed were the trade wind routes—sea lanes where the wind would be at their backs.

Even at Op-Sail, the majority of boats could

sail only 60 degrees to the apparent wind (the direction the wind appears to blow when you're aboard a moving boat). This was like going back and forth in sideways directions to move ahead to a destination.

With today's changes in styles of boats, in riggings, in sails, the *points of sailing*—a sailboat's directional heading in relation to the wind—are a science and an art that must be understood for more efficient sailing. Points of sailing are like the gears on an automobile. To drive a car properly, you must know what gear to use. To sail a boat properly, you must know the position of the boom in relation to the wind—that is the point of sailing.

There are three main categories of the POINTS OF SAILING: *beating, reaching,* and *running.*

Beating—sailing as close to the wind as possible, also referred to as *close haul, sailing to windward, tacking to windward.* It is the most exciting and also the wettest of the points of sailing. No boat can sail directly into the wind, but you come as close to the wind as possible. Generally, you will be able to get to 45 degrees of the direction from which the wind is blowing. Then the sails will luff (flap), and drive will be lost if you sail closer.

What actually happens in beating is as follows: The sails are trimmed quite flat, as far as they will

Luffing—poor sailing ability create this mess.

Driving and sailing properly—a perfect example, as opposed to luffing.

go, 10 degrees or less off the boat's centerline. The leech of the sail is hardened. You should keep the leeches of the jib and the mainsail about parallel to each other. The jib should be adjusted so that it will luff just before the mainsail luffs. If the luff of the mainsail flutters, it means you are heading up into the wind too much. Ideal position is a boat pointing so that the jib barely luffs with each new wind shift.

An old sailing expression best sums up the problem in beating: "Full-and-by." It means you keep the sails full, steer a course as close by the wind as possible.

Beating is not the most desirable point of sailing to be in unless you have to be there. The boat heels in this position more than in any other point of sailing, and there is more pressure on the boat. If you have passengers who are newcomers to sailing, they may get petrified from the dramatic dips of the boat toward the water and the heeling. Beating is fun; it can be the best position in light air. Could be employed only when you are heading somewhere, not when you are just lolling about on the water.

Reaching—sailing across the wind. *Close reaching, beam reaching,* and *broad reaching* are three positions of reaching. This point of sailing is between beating and running. It is a good position for the beginning sailor to practice. Reaching com-

IN THE GROOVE
Going to weather in 18 knots looks great. Heeling 17 degrees.

IN THE GROOVE
Looking great with perfect form on a close reach.

IN THE GROOVE

Great-looking jib leech; main looks good—heel 12 degrees—fine for close haul. At these settings you will get optimum speed going to weather.

bines both the lift and the push of the wind. With a good wind, light, flat-bottomed boats can lift out of the water and plane. Sailing in the reaching position makes you most aware of the rolling motion of the waves. There is also less resistance to the forward movement of the boat by the water than there is in other positions.

Close reach—between beating and beam reaching—takes place when you are sailing directly across the wind at an angle more than that of close-hauled. Trim the sails quite flat as far as they will go, within 27 degrees or less of the boat's center-line. Generally you'll be in the fastest point of sail-ing. By easing the sheet or the traveler, you get the sail farther away from the centerline, increasing forward drive.

Beam reach is the position where you are sail-ing slightly with the wind when it is nearly directly abeam (the maximum width point of the boat from side to side). When the wind moves the beam per-pendicular to the fore and aft centerline of the boat, you should ease the boom as far as you can until sails begin luffing. Bring the boom back or in until luffing stops. You now have perfect position, with the wind at a 90-degree angle to the boat's center-line.

Broad reach is the position between a beam

Beam reach—boat is being sailed extremely fast and flat. Crew weight placed as far aft as possible to keep bow high.

reach and a run. The wind is actually between 90 and 135 degrees to the boat. Ease the boom position as far forward as rigging will permit, 90 degrees or at right angles to the apparent wind.

Running—sailing before the wind. This is perhaps the least exciting point of sailing. The speed and the responsiveness of the boat are lessened. What actually is happening is that you are sailing downwind before the wind, and the apparent wind is much lighter because you are sailing away from the wind. You are trying to get as much of the wind's push as possible by getting it to push squarely against the greatest possible sail area. The sail is pushed along by the wind, and at the same time it makes its own resistance.

The mechanics of running are as follows: Ease the mainsail sheet until the boom is well out from the boat on one side, with the wind coming across the stern from the other. Ease sheets until sails are at right angles to the wind. It is very important that you carefully observe the wind position from astern. A shift in wind might come around just enough to slam your sail across the boat to the other side—a condition known as jibing. With more experience in running, you'll learn to "wing by wing." This is spreading the jib to the side of the boat opposite to the mainsail.

Note effective boom vang setting to close leech and main. Jib sheet is inboard. At this point of sail, it would be more effective if jib fairlead was placed on outboard track.

Full and quarter run: In the full run the boom position should be eased as far forward as rigging will permit, no farther than 90 degrees to the apparent wind. In the quarter run, the position of the wind is slightly off the corner of the boat, in a 15- to 20-degree angle.

THE TRAVELER AND BOOM VANG: POINTS OF SAILING AIDS

Both the traveler and boom vang provide extra measures of safety and efficiency in sailing. The traveler repositions the boom without the need on your part to ease the main sheet. It takes over and gives control to the boom when the sheet is in its farthest extended position. The greatest benefit of the traveler comes under erratic and puffy wind conditions. The traveler can be eased out to spill air and keep the boat from heeling (tipping).

When the sheet is eased and the traveler is in its farthest leeward position, the boom vang is used to keep the boom from assuming an upward position, not parallel to the waterline. In the full run position, the boom vang can prevent accidental jibes, and it keeps the mainsail flat. In broad and beam reach positions, the boom vang prevents the upper end of the sail from opening so much that air is spilled. It thereby contributes to sailing efficiency.

STEERING AND THE TILLER

A leverlike stick attached to the top of the rudder post, the tiller in many ways is like the steering wheel of an automobile. The tiller has been called the heart and the lifeblood of a boat. The great thrill of sailing comes from the feel of the stick, the tiller, in your hand. Nature tells you things through the tiller. It is your link with the water, the wind, the moods of nature that can change in a moment. With your hand on the tiller you and the water and the wind become one.

There are a few basic principles affecting the use of the tiller. One tricky concept to master is that to move the boat to the right, you move the tiller to the left. To move the boat to the left, you move the tiller to the right. A second basic principle is always to keep your tiller hand in the "neutral" position. You can move your head and your eyes to the left and the right, but don't move the tiller along with them unless you want to move the boat.

Third, remember that whatever the angle the tiller is at in your hand, under the boat in the form of the rudder there's a corresponding angle in the water. The more acute the angle, the more resistance you're creating, the more drag. Sensitivity to the tiller position helps you reduce the angle and reduce the drag. Remember—if you're struggling to move the tiller, you're creating a barrier against the water. This puts more pressure on the sails and slows down the boat.

A fourth important principle is that, in all points of sailing, the tiller should be a maximum of 5 degrees off the centerline of the boat (this is something to attempt, although it may be difficult or impossible in strong winds). That's why two boats of the same design both with excellent sailors can go at different speeds. One boat may sail with a helm of 4 degrees and the other with 7 degrees. The 3-degree differential in the rudder will make one boat go much faster than the other.

A fifth principle of tillering is that you should never oversteer. Inefficient sailing is sailing that constantly readjusts tiller position. You should be relaxed and in control. Keep the tiller as close to the centerline as possible at all times, but don't be so overly sensitive that you're mentally measuring and physically playing with the tiller. The main purpose of the tiller is to keep the boat on an even keel—even-keeled sailors make for even-keeled boats.

We suggest that you add a tiller extension to your tiller. It is a simple attachment to the tiller that allows you more mobility. You can hike (sit) out on the boat and still control the tiller, and you also have the ability to swing the tiller extension either way.

TURNING MANEUVERS: TACKING AND JIBING

Tacking and jibing are both turning maneuvers. Tacking is changing course in an upwind direction by bringing your bow into and through the wind's eye. Jibing is changing course in a downwind direction by bringing your stern into and through the wind's eye.

Since a boat can arrive at a point directly upwind diagonally, tacking or slanting maneuvers are necessary. Tacking enables the boat to get from place to place, to avoid other boats, to avoid rocks or other obstacles. In practice, it's "playing the wind" by steering the boat into the wind, past it, and over to its other side. When you tack, the front or bow of the boat is passing through the eye of the

Tacking (port to starboard).

Tacking (port to starboard) jib passing through slot.

Tacking (port to starboard) beginning to drive on new tack and almost "sheeted home."

wind. For example, if the wind is coming from the right side (starboard), you turn the boat to the right until the wind comes from the left (port). In order to sail on, the wind has to come from the new side at an angle of 45 degrees.

Tacking smoothly is an art that is learned through experience. If you push the rudder far over very quickly, the rudder becomes a brake rather than a steering device. If you move the rudder too timidly, the result can be a boat that loses momentum before the turn is completed because the radius is too long.

Jibing is used for quicker changes of course than tacking. If there is a choice between jibing and tacking, always tack.

Jibing puts tremendous pressure on the sails and the rigging. Jibing pressure is created by having the boom swing from one tack to the other a full 180 degrees. You are actually stopping a sail that could be traveling 50 miles per hour in a matter of inches. So jibe only if you have to, and avoid doing it except in the lightest of air.

Accomplished under any point of sailing to another point of sailing, jibing takes place only when the boat is pointing downwind. Just before jibing, the mainsheet is hauled in. The tighter the mainsheet can be hauled in, the less the boom swinging distance will be, and the safer is the jibe.

Shouted commands help make the jibe safer. "Stand by to jibe." This alerts the crew to man stations and duck heads to avoid the swinging boom. The boat is held before the wind. The wind catches behind the mainsail, and the whole mainsail and the boom swing in a total arc to the other side of the boat. That's your jibe. You yell "Jibe ho" loud, so that everybody can hear and duck.

The tiller is moved away from the sail. You straighten the helm and slack the mainsheet quickly, and steer on a new course, trimming the jib. Crew weight is shifted for balance and safety.

If the jibe is planned and properly executed, there is no problem. An unplanned or accidental jibe can be disastrous. You can get hit by the boom, fall off the boat, suffer severe physical damage. Jibing almost symbolizes an important part of sailing— respect for the sea and the boat and yourself. If you know what you're doing, you'll know what sailing is all about.

In sum, sailing is both an art and a science. You now should have a pretty good idea of the science of sailing and a feel for the art form that is sailing. Put the principles of this chapter to work, and you'll be on your way to being a sailing artist and a scientific sailor.

Points of Sailing—
Summary Comments

BEATING (CLOSE HAUL, TO WEATHER, ON WIND)

Set main as close to boat's centerline as weather permits. Ease boom to reduce heeling if desired, realizing boat will not point as high.

CLOSE REACH

Ease boom approximately 10 to 20 degrees. Stop when mainsail luffs. Then bring in main (boom and mainsheet) until luffing stops. The same procedure applies for jib. Reduced heeling will take place along with generally faster sailing.

BEAM REACH

Ease out main and jib to about 60 degrees off boat's centerline. Use the luffing technique for both jib and main. Most flat-bottom boats will plane in moderate and heavy winds. There will be very fast sailing. A boom vang should be used.

BROAD REACH

Both boom and jib should be eased out at right angles to the wind. In heavy air, this is the fast form of sailing because of planing. Use boom vang.

QUARTER RUN AND RUN

Boom should be 65 degrees off boat's centerline in quarter run. Comments dealing with broad reach apply to quarter run and run. Boom should be 90° off boat's centerline for full run.

4. Sailing with the Senses

THE FIVE SENSES AND SAILING

Much of sailing comes through the senses. The more you sail, the more sensitive your senses will become. You can hear and see, feel and smell and even taste your way to greater sensitivity as a sailor. Your ears can make you aware of the sounds water changes make at the bow, the stern, the bottom of the boat. Rigging sounds also bring a message. An extremely luffing boat creates its own racket—sails shaking or slapping back and forth near the mast.

Your eyes can study telltales, the wake, the horizon, other boats. Your eyes bring a message to

63

you about the proper way to operate on the water.

Through your sense of balance your body can feel the rise and dip of a boat. Luffing makes a boat come more upright. A boat "on the wind" heels a lot. Pressure of the body can be increased or reduced against the cockpit or railing to make a boat become more upright or heel more or heel less.

Your fingertip touch on the tiller gives you a great feel of the way the water and the boat are reacting to each other. Increased or reduced pressure of water past the rudder can be felt in the tiller.

Wind pressure can be felt and almost tasted as it increases or lessens against your body. This is another sense impression of sailing.

POINTS OF SAIL.

Sailing on a beam reach in 20–25 knots of wind. Note windex on top of mast showing wind from starboard beam. Boom is eased. All telltales are flat except at lower middle. This reveals the negative force at the back end of the sail that could be corrected by using outboard genoa track for sheeting.

WEATHER AND BAROMETRIC PRESSURE
SIGNS FOR THE SENSES

There are also tips to the senses that come from observation of the sky, the wind, the clouds, barometric pressure readings that will help your sailing sensitivity.

1. A barometric pressure rise when the wind is coming from the northwest indicates that weather will be dry and wind will be diminishing.

2. A barometric pressure fall when the wind is coming from the southwest indicates wet weather and a lot of wind.

3. If the wind swings to the west, in all probability it will be short-lived and will swing back to where it came from originally.

4. When barometric pressure has been very low and then it rises, you will have some very strong winds.

5. If conditions are very dramatic—cloudy and windy—over a long period and there is no rain, chances are you're going to have a storm with a lot of rain, and it will last a long while. ''Long

66

foretold—long last.''

6. ''Short notice—soon will pass.'' Many times in squalls, winds of possibly 30 to 40 knots develop. These winds come on short notice, but they can last an hour.

7. A rapid and considerable barometer rise indicates unsettled weather.

8. A rapid barometer fall indicates stormy weather.

9. The greatest depressions or falls in barometric pressure come from gales from the southeast or southwest. The greatest elevations come from winds from the northwest, north, or northeast.

10. Winds coming from the west with a sudden drop in barometric pressure may indicate a violent storm is brewing.

BALANCE: HULL AND CREW

Balance on a sailboat is a very important part of efficient and safe sailing. Hull balance is the way the boat rides on the water as a result of what the designer puts into the boat. You can't change hull balance, but you can modify it. Crew balance is what the members of a boat can do by positioning themselves to modify the balance of the boat.

A very important aspect of balance is the weather rail. In heavier wind conditions, all crew weight should be moved to the side the wind is coming from to reduce the amount of heeling. The crew becomes movable ballast (weight). The crew members are actually seated as close to the beam as possible at the windward rail, which is referred to as the weather rail.

A weather helm is the tendency of a boat to steer toward the wind. A slight weather helm is a desirable thing as opposed to a neutral helm, which is not responsive. With the slight weather helm and increased wind, you get the feel of the sea. To determine the helm balance, release the tiller. The probability is that the boat will head upwind, indicating that you have a good weather helm. Raking or inclining the mast fore or aft will change helm balance.

Crew balance has an effect on helm balance. Placing crew members at the bow of the boat will increase helm and make for a stronger weather helm.

Certain Basic Crew Balance Positions
That Should Be Observed:

LIGHT AIR:

Point of Sailing	Crew Position
run	center amidship or at the bow
quarter run	lee aft
beam reach	center amidship
close reach	lee center
broad reach	center amidship
close haul	leeward rail amidship or at the bow

It is best to have a 2° to 6° weather helm in light air.

HEAVY AIR:

Point of Sailing	Crew Position
run	windward aft
quarter run	center aft
beam reach	windward aft
close reach	windward
broad reach	windward aft
close haul	weather rail amidship

ARTISTIC-LOOKING BUT IMPROPER SAILING WITH THE SENSES.
Boat under spinnaker looks good, but pole could come down or the spinnaker sheet coul
be eased. Both clews of the spinnaker must be the same height.

BALANCE VIA THE MAINSHEET, TRAVELER, AND JIB

Effective balance through the weather helm and positioning the crew may not be enough under some conditions. The weather helm may be too strong. You may get a feeling that the boat will tip. There are three other balancing procedures that you can use.

1. Ease the sheet—the sail may not be perfectly aligned, but you'll go faster, flatter, safer.

2. Ease the traveler—this approach will also help to spill wind. A combination of sheet and traveler easing may also be used.

3. Drive with the jib—if conditions become such that you must take added precautions to spill more air, move the jib fairlead (an eye or casting holding a line) farther aft to open up the jib leech (aft side of sail) at the top. This should get you on the right track.

71

A *Backstay adjuster.*   B *Reef in main.*   C *Telltales on main and jib and telltale win-*
dow.

SHAPING OF SAILS

Sensitivity to wind is a sensory experience of all sailors. Just as weather helm is built into the body of a boat, draft is built into the sails of a boat. Draft is the depth of a sail from the deepest point of its curve to an imaginary line drawn from its tack to its clew (its two bottom corners). Draft, aerodynamics, position of fairlead, halyard tension—all of these affect boat speed and safety. You should be aware that under different wind conditions, different procedures are necessary.

Wind 0–2 Knots

In this wind condition, you should induce heeling. Position the crew lee amidship. Trim the boom well out until the boat gains speed; then move it to centerline or weather. If the draft in the main is medium, pick the forward end of the boom up. With a very slight twist in the main, the draft should be full up high. Light battens should be used.

The jib fairlead should be forward for full draft,

73

SAILING WITH THE SENSES.

Look at the four marks (tape) on the spreader. This can allow you to position the jib at th
spot that is best for the wind and speed conditions you are sailing under. Each one of th
four marks is at a location about 3 inches from the other.

18 percent or two feet from the track to check depth of draft in jib. As with the main, the top of the sail should be full. The jib should be sheeted inboard with an open leech. The sail should be three inches off the spreader (a device that spreads the rigging to strengthen the mast). There should be an easing of the jib halyard and backstay.

Set the sails as follows: Luff up the boat to check jib luff telltales; set the fairlead so that all telltales break at the same time when luffing up. Once this is checked, look at the leech of the jib, then ease the jib sheet till the top leech telltale breaks. Then bring in the sheet until it stops flapping. It is worth noting that in light air, chop, and waves, both mainsail and jib should be open, with big full draft.

Wind 2–5 Knots

In this wind condition, you should follow the same procedures as for 0–2 knots, except you should have the boom toward weather. In smooth water, luff tension is eased on the jib but the backstay is tightened. Use a relatively tight leech on the main and use light battens. Ease curves in the leech of the jib. Induce heel and sail by the flickering or limp telltales (stalls).

Wind 5–9 Knots

The same procedures as in winds of 2–5 knots apply here with a couple of exceptions. The jib should be flatter, with the twist reduced. The traveler should be eased until the main backwinds. Play the main only to point high.

Wind 8–10 knots

Play both main traveler and jib sheets to point high. Sail by the luff telltale. Ease traveler till maximum heel is reached. The twist and the draft should be reduced to a moderate 10% to 12%. In puffs, feather boat to point high—you'll actually be sailing by luffing. There should be a maximum helm of 5% and heavy battens should be used. To get high pointing ability, try inboard sheeting of jib. Set the jib and main by checking both luff and leech telltales.

Wind 9–13 Knots

Open the leech in the jib. Move the fairlead aft, and at the same time sheet the jib to the outboard track. Put a twist in the main. If the helm is more than 5 degrees off the centerline, ease the traveler until the main backwinds. Then tighten the mainsheet until the backwinding stops. If the boat is heeling more than 25 degrees, reef the main. Then check the helm to maintain a course no more than 5 degrees off centerline. Increase luff tension in the jib to move the draft forward by tightening the jib halyard. Use tension in the Cunningham rope to move the draft in the main forward. The jib should be six to twelve inches off the spreader from top to bottom. The crew should be positioned windward aft.

Wind 13–18 Knots

Apply the same procedures as in 9 to 13 knots. Ease the traveler. Increase twist up high in both the main and jib sails. If pointing is unsatisfactory, provide more twist by further easing of main and jib sheets.

Wind 18–25 Knots

Apply the same procedures as in 13 to 18 knots. Ease the traveler all the way. Keep the twist in the jib.

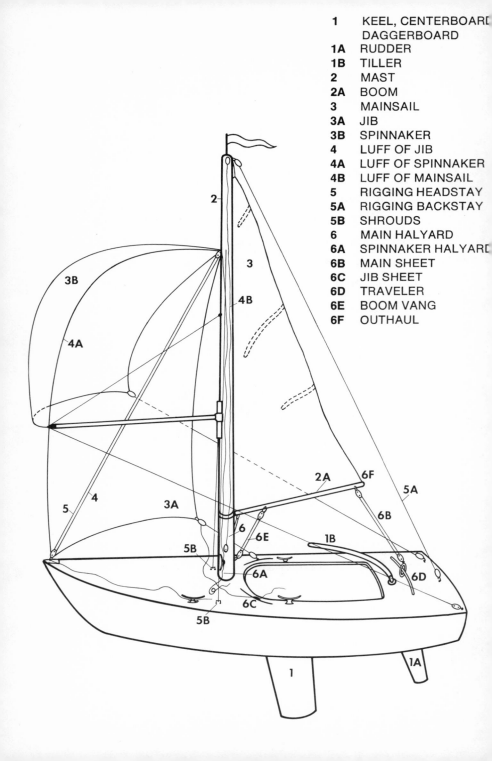

1   KEEL, CENTERBOARD DAGGERBOARD
1A RUDDER
1B TILLER
2   MAST
2A BOOM
3   MAINSAIL
3A JIB
3B SPINNAKER
4   LUFF OF JIB
4A LUFF OF SPINNAKER
4B LUFF OF MAINSAIL
5   RIGGING HEADSTAY
5A RIGGING BACKSTAY
5B SHROUDS
6   MAIN HALYARD
6A SPINNAKER HALYARD
6B MAIN SHEET
6C JIB SHEET
6D TRAVELER
6E BOOM VANG
6F OUTHAUL

DRAFT POSITIONS

Main Sail

Knots	*% of Draft**			
0–2	45	50	50	55
2–5	45	50	50	55
5–9	40	45	45	50
10–25	35	40	40	45

Jib Sail

0–2	50 aft
2–5	45 aft
5–9	37 aft
10–25	35 aft

* % figures refer to the placement of draft from the top to the bottom of the sail, divided into four equal parts.

BAROMETER READING	PROBABLE WEATHER CONDITIONS

BAROMETER RISING

28.8 to 29.2	clearing, high winds and cool wave
29.2 to 29.6	high winds, cool wave (squalls)
29.6 to 29.9	fair, fresh winds for 24 hours
29.9 to 30.2	fair, brisk winds diminishing
30.2 to 30.5	fair, cooler, variable winds
30.5 to 30.8	continued cool, clear, light wind
30.8 to 31.0	high wind southeast with rain

BAROMETER FALLING

30.8 to 30.5	fair, warmer, followed by rain
30.5 to 30.2	approaching storm
30.2 to 29.9	cloudy, warmer, unsettled
29.9 to 29.6	unsettled, increasing wind
29.6 to 29.3	squally, clearing, cooler weather
29.3 to 29.0	high winds, squalls, cooler
29.0 to 28.7	stormy weather

5. Tips from the Pros

NOW THAT YOU'VE gotten this far in the book, we are going to treat you to some rare and exotic information. Some of the following ideas and approaches are rumored to be closely guarded secrets of champion sailors who do not normally share their winning techniques. Some of the tips are obvious ways of doing things, but they're presented in a concise fashion so that you'll be able to remember and apply them to your sailing.

    1. To achieve high pointing ability if the boat is set up with an inboard and an outboard track keep the clew as close to the centerline as possible. When the boat goes off wind, position the jib fairlead to

the outboard track for better sail shape.

2. To sail more effectively to weather (close haul) in light air, crew weight should not only be to leeward side but slightly forward of mast. By dipping the bow you reduce the wettest surface of the hull, picking the stern out of the water, reducing hull friction, creating an additional weather helm. This procedure will make the boat go much faster than another vessel not under the same procedure.

3. To increase boat speed on a beam reach, run the jib sheet through the after end of the boom in a turning block. The jib clew is further extended from the boat centerline and the boat gets more thrust.

4. A crew member can become a human boom vang when a boat is lacking this piece of equipment. Simply get a crew member to sit on the boom. This can help prevent an accidental jibe.

5. In extremely light air, concentrate crew weight at the centerline approximately at the base of the mast slightly forward of normal off-wind work. As the wind or puffs hit, fall off or sail lower, because the extra speed makes the wind move aft.

6. Slatting is a condition under close haul, close reach, beam reach, where the chop is immense and the wind is light. The jib bobs up and down spilling air. Placing your hand on the foot of the jib and holding it in a fixed position will increase con-

trol, speed, and safety of the boat.

7. In the lightest of air, strive for baggy sails. Get the boom 5 to 10 degrees to weather of centerline—not leeward. This creates a curved shape in main that should increase boat speed. But in 0–1 knots, ease boom to leeward about 30°.

8. In going to weather, secure the jib headstay as tight as possible. For each wind speed, use the draft position chart. This makes for greater speed and pointing ability (but not in chop and not on a reach or off-wind sailing).

9. If possible, equip your boat with a backstay adjuster for control of fullness and flatness of mainsail.

10. Equip all your sails with telltales to help you more easily determine the true and apparent wind direction. When the telltales are flat on both sides of the sail, both the main and jib are in proper position. When a telltale flickers or goes limp, this indicates that sails are stalling. The use of telltales at the batten aft end will indicate main sheet, vang, traveler are set in proper position if all are flat and flowing aft.

11. Different points of sailing should make you rely on different telltales. When reaching, close reaching, you should sail by the luff telltales flat. On a beam reach sail by the luff telltales stalling with no

Outside telltales are straight, indicating boat is being sailed by the luff. (Photo taken in 35 m.p.h. winds which made feathering necessary.)

Both outside and inside telltales in stalled position, indicating improper point of sail.

twist in the mainsail.

12. Strive for an attitude of planing whenever possible. Boat speed can be tremendously increased. Recognize that planing can't be reached in close haul but that it is possible in close reach. Keep the boat flat and trim the sails properly. Keep the bottom clean. You will plane in most small boats if the wind is great.

13. Strive for the proper angle of attack in the varied points of sailing:

CLOSE HAUL: position of the boom 3 to 7 degrees to weather or lee of center off the centerline of the boat. Jib is as close to the centerline as possible. Prevent luffing.

CLOSE REACH: boom 12 to 27 degrees to leeward. The jib fairlead is changed to outboard tracks. Jib should be eased until luffing begins. Jib should then be eased back until luffing stops. Jib halyard should be eased to move draft in jib aft.

BEAM REACH: boom position 60 degrees off centerline. Use boom vang for tightening leech. The position of the draft should be moved as far aft as possible. (Ease jib halyard and use vang.)

BROAD REACH: boom is moved as far forward as rigging permits. If a spinnaker is used, its pole should be at right angles to the wind. (Ease jib halyard and use vang.)

QUARTER RUN: boom is 65 degrees off centerline, not 90. Jib and spinnaker position is similar to broad reach.

FULL RUN: boom is positioned at right angles to the wind. Caution should be taken not to cause accidental jibe. For more speed heel boat to weather.

14. Proper centerboard placement in the different points of sailing should follow this pattern:

—When going to weather in moderate or heavy air, the board should be all the way down.

—In lighter airs, the board should be down three-quarters of the way.

In close reach, the board should be down three-quarters of the way in light and heavy air. In beam reach, broad reach, and quarter run, the board should be halfway down. In full run, there is no need for the board. It could be all the way up.

15. When you sail with a spinnaker on a beam reach, the pole should be 5 degrees to 10 degrees off the headstay in winds over 10 knots. It can be on the headstay in lighter winds.

16. When tacking, ease main sheet to open leech about 10 percent in light and heavy air. By following this procedure, you'll be able to tack with more speed.

Glossary

ABAFT Toward the stern.

ABEAM At right angles to the boat's centerline.

AFT Toward the back of the boat, the stern.

AMIDSHIPS The center of the boat, midway between the bow and the stern, midway between the sides.

BACKSTAYS Lines from the mast to the stern that secure the mast.

BALLAST Weight at the lowest point of the boat for purposes of stabilization. "Outside ballast" is lead or iron weight in the keel. "Inside ballast" is movable weights inside the boat.

BATTEN Strip of plastic or wood that stiffens the roach in a sail's leech.

Batten Pocket   Pocket that holds batten.

Beam   The width of the boat.

Bear Off   To turn downwind, away from the wind.

Beat   To sail to windward.

Bend   To make a sail fast to a spar through use of knots, hooks, grooves, slides, etc.

Bilge   The turn of the hull below the waterline; also the area where water collects inside the hull.

Bitter End   The free end of a rope used for fastening.

Block   Pulley.

Boom   The spar at the bottom of a sail at right angles to the mast.

Bow   The front end of a boat.

Bridle   A length of wire fastened at both ends and pulled at some point within its length.

Broach   To swing sharply toward wind when running due to poor steering, heavy seas, and heavy wind.

Bumpers   Protectors on boat's side from docks, piles, other boats, etc.

Burdened Vessel   Vessel that does not have right of way.

Centerboard   A device located on the centerline of boats without permanent keels that can be lowered to navigate in shallow waters or to secure against a sideward slip.

CENTERLINE The center of a boat from bow to stern.

CHAIN PLATES Metal plates bolted to side of boat to hold shrouds and stays.

CHARTS Nautical maps that contain navigation aids, water depths, landmarks, etc.

CHOCK A casting of metal or plastic through which lines are led to other vessels or to shore and which guard these lines against chafing.

CLEAT A metal, plastic, or wood device that holds a line secure.

CLEW The lower aft corner of a triangular sail.

CLOSE-HAULED As close as possible to the wind with sails trimmed for beating. Also known as "on the wind," "beating," "strapped down."

COAMING A raised frame for protection around the cockpit.

COCKPIT The portion of the boat for the crew to sail and sit in.

CRINGLE An eye of metal threaded into a sail for securing purposes.

DAGGER BOARD A movable stiff device at boat's centerline used to avoid leeway.

DECK PLATE A plate bolted to the deck, usually with an eye for shackles or blocks.

Downhaul   A rope or rope/block that pulls down the boom to tighten the luffs.

Draft   (1) The deepest point of a sail from the depth of its curve to an imaginary line drawn from its tack to its clew (its two bottom corners). (2) The distance from a boat's waterline to the bottom of its hull or keel.

Ease   To relieve the pressure on a sail by letting out the sheet.

Eye Splice   A splice making the end of a rope into a loop.

Fairlead   An eye or casting that guides a line where a block is not needed.

Fetch   Verb: To reach a goal without coming about. Noun: Distance free from obstruction of tide or wind.

Fly   A masthead pennant or piece of yarn in rigging to indicate apparent wind.

Foot   Lower edge of a sail.

Fore, Forward   To the front.

Free   Sailing with the wind anywhere from abeam to directly behind.

Freeboard   Vertical distance from waterline to deck.

Furl   To wrap a sail to a spar.

Gooseneck   A jointed fitting that secures boom to mast.

HALYARD Rope or wire for raising and lowering sails.

HARD ALEE Short for "The helm is hard alee," which is the signal for the movement of the rudder incident to turning.

HEAD (1) Upper corner of a triangular sail. (2) A boat's toilet.

HEADBOARD A wood or plastic stiffener used in the head of a sail.

HEADSTAYS Lines from the mast to the bow that secure the mast.

HEAD TO WIND Sails shaking as the boat heads into wind, luffing.

HEADWAY Forward motion.

HEAVE Verb: To throw or cast, to pull on a rope. Noun: The rise and fall of a vessel.

HEEL To tip or tilt.

HELM (1) The lever that controls the rudder. (2) The tendency of a vessel to steer relative to the wind; "weather helm" means tending to steer toward the wind.

HULL The body of a boat exclusive of rigging, centerboard, etc.

IN IRONS or IN STAYS A condition in which the boat faces into the wind and has lost all headway.

JIB A triangular sail in front of the mast.

JIBE To change tacks by turning away from the

wind toward the sail.

JIB-HEADED   A triangular sail; also called Marconi, Bermudian.

JIB STAY   Stay that raises jib.

JUMPER STRUT   A device on front side of mast to increase stability of upper part of mast.

KEEL   Backbone of a boat; also a fixed extension at bottom of boat for greater stability.

KNOT   (1) Friction device to keep line from slipping. (2) A nautical measure of speed. One knot means one nautical mile per hour. (A nautical mile is equal to one minute of latitude or longitude, and is 1.15 statute miles.)

LANYARD   A short, light line for temporary ties.

LAYLINE   The line on which a boat can fetch a mark or buoy.

LEECH   The aft edge of a sail.

LEE   Opposite to windward, the side of anything away from the wind. A lee shore is the shore at which the wind blows. "Leeward" means toward the lee side.

LEEWAY   Distance slipped to leeward.

LINES   Ropes or wires used in rigging.

LIST   Leaning of vessel to heavier side.

LUFF   The fore edge of a sail.

LUFFING   Shaking of sail when its head is toward the wind.

Mainmast The sole mast of a one-masted boat; the principal mast of a boat with more than one mast.

Mainsail Sail rigged on the back of the mainmast.

Mainsheet Line used to control mainsail.

Make Fast To tie up, secure.

Mast A vertical spar on which sails are hoisted.

Moor To secure to a mooring.

Mooring An anchorage for securing a boat in water so that it is free to move in a complete circle.

Offshore Away from shore.

Off the Wind Sailing other than a close-hauled course.

On the Wind Sailing a close-hauled course.

Outboard Beyond the hull.

Outhaul Rope used to secure foot of sail.

Overstand To go beyond the layline unnecessarily.

Pay Off, Pay Out (1) To ease out a length of line. (2) To turn the bow away from the wind.

Pendant A short piece of line used for securing.

Pennant A triangular flag.

Pinch To sail a boat inefficiently close to the wind.

Point To head high, close to the wind.

Port Left.

Port Tack Sailing with the wind from the port (left) side.

Privileged Vessel Vessel with right of way.

Quarter The boat's side between the beam and the stern.

Rail A light guard structure on the outer edge of deck.

Rake Inclination of mast toward fore and aft.

Reach Sailing course between close-hauled and running.

Ready About! Spoken signal to prepare for tacking.

Reef To make a sail smaller or reduce sail area.

Reeve To pass a line through a block or fairlead.

Rig Boat's sail plan and mast arrangement.

Rigging Spars, sails, sheets, blocks, etc. Standing rigging is permanent. Running rigging can be moved about.

Roach The curve in the foot, leech, or luff of a sail.

Rode Anchor line.

Run (1) To sail almost directly before the wind. (2) The aft underwater shape of the hull.

Sail Stops Straps used to tie a sail to a spar.

Sea Cocks Safety devices placed at or below waterline to control water flow in or out of boat.

Seaway Sea area.

SHACKLE   U-shaped metal fitting that joins two objects.

SHEAVE   The wheel in a block (pulley).

SHEET   A rope used to control a sail.

SLIP   A docking area between two small piers or floating booms.

SNAP **H**OOKS   Hooks that spring closed.

SOLE   The floor of the boat's cabin.

SPAR   Pole.

SPINNAKER   Large, lightweight sail used for reaching or running.

SPREADER   Device to spread rigging for increased strength in offsetting tendency of mast to bend.

STARBOARD   Right.

STARBOARD **T**ACK   Sailing with the wind from the starboard (right) side.

STAYS   Lines that support mast.

STEM   The foremost part of a boat at the bow.

STERNWAY   Backward motion.

STOPS   Straps used to secure sail to boom.

TACK   (1) The forward corner of a sail. (2) Noun: A forward course. Verb: To change from one course to another as opposed to jibing.

TENDER   (1) Lacking stiffness, lacking tendency to heel. (2) Dinghylike craft to transport supplies or people from shore to boat.

TILLER   Wooden lever used to move the rudder.

TOPSIDES The sides of a boat above the waterline.

TRANSOM A broad, nearly vertical stern.

TRAVELER A horizontal track near the stern with a slide runing on it that is fastened to the mainsheet. The traveler enables the sheet to move from one side to the other when the boat is tacked, increasing sailing efficiency.

TRIM Verb: To adjust a sail relative to wind direction and course of boat. Noun: The balance of a boat.

TURNBUCKLE A threaded link that pulls two devices together. Used to adjust tension in stays and shrouds.

WAKE Disturbance in the water caused by drag or resistance of vessel as it passes through water.

WATERLINE Dividing line between topsides and underbody of boat.

WHISKER POLE Light pole used to hold a jib to windward so that it may fill with wind.

WINCH Small, drum-shaped device used to increase mechanical advantage for pulling in a line against tension; line is wound clockwise, three turns or more.

WINDWARD, WEATHER Toward the wind; opposite of leeward.

WORKING SAILS Ordinary sails as opposed to light or storm sails.

About the Authors

HARVEY FROMMER authored *A Baseball Century: 100 Years of the National League.* A former sports writer for United Press, he currently is a professor of communications in the City University of New York. Long an observer of the sports-cultural scene, Dr. Frommer's Ph.D. thesis investigated the relationship of television and professional sports. His newest work, *The Martial Arts Book: Judo and Karate,* will be published by Atheneum late in 1978.

RON WEINMANN is a self-taught sailor who mastered the art of sailing in three years. He has won twenty-nine trophies in three years of difficult racing competition. Out of the water, Mr. Weinmann is an account executive for a national printing firm. Ron is a member of Sheldrake Yacht Club, Yacht Racing Association of Long Island Sound, Midget Ocean Racing Conference, Performance Handicap Racing Federation.